dabblelab

EPIC CARDBOARD ADVENTURES

TRAVEL THROUGH TIME WITH CARDBOARD (& DUCT TAPE)

BY
LESLIE MANLAPIG

4D™
AN AUGMENTED READING CARDBOARD EXPERIENCE

CAPSTONE PRESS
a capstone imprint

TABLE OF CONTENTS

Download the Capstone 4D app!

STEP 1 Ask an adult to search in the Apple App Store or Google Play for "Capstone 4D".

STEP 2 Click Install (Android) or Get, then Install (Apple).

STEP 3 Open the app.

STEP 4 Scan any of the following spreads with this icon:

Watch some fun videos!

When you scan a spread, you'll find fun extra stuff to go with this book! You can also find these things on the web at www.capstone4D.com using the password: cardboard.travel

YOUR ADVENTURE STARTS
↓ HERE ↓↓

Have you dreamed of traveling through time? This book will help you do that and more using . . .

CARDBOARD!

⟩ Yes, that's right! ⟨

The boxes sitting around your house can be used to make your very own adventures. All you need are some simple supplies and a willing adult helper to help you with sharp tools.

Don't forget to check out the 4D videos to help guide you through the steps. Also, we've included many templates to help you complete projects in this book. Just scan this star!
Before you know it, you'll be stomping with dinos and sailing the high seas!

SUPPLIES

hammer and nails (or a drill) to make holes

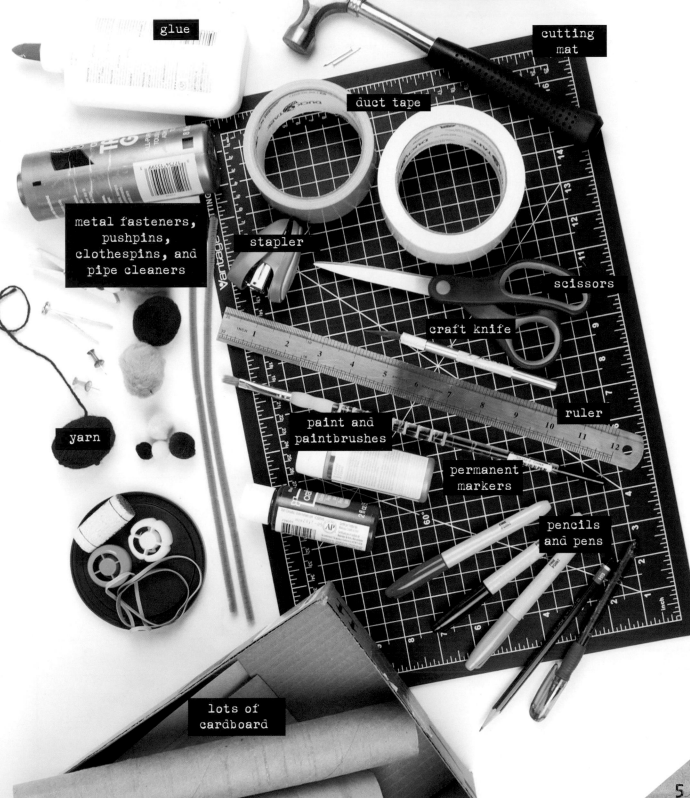

glue

cutting mat

duct tape

metal fasteners, pushpins, clothespins, and pipe cleaners

stapler

scissors

craft knife

ruler

paint and paintbrushes

yarn

permanent markers

pencils and pens

lots of cardboard

DINOSAURS

What would it be like to live during the time of dinosaurs? Hop into your time machine and find out!

SUPPLIES

- corrugated cardboard
- scissors
- drill
- paint and paintbrush
- permanent markers
- metal fasteners

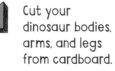 Cut your dinosaur bodies, arms, and legs from cardboard.

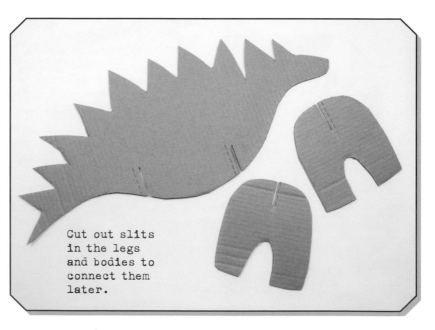

Cut out slits in the legs and bodies to connect them later.

2 Drill a hole through each arm and dinosaur body to make arms that move.

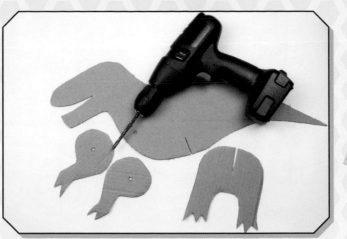

3 Paint your dinosaurs. Use markers to add extra details that make your prehistoric beasts pop.

For a fun contrast, try painting one side like a skeleton and the other side normally.

4 Fasten the arms to the bodies. Slide the leg pieces in. You're all set!

PROJECT #2
PTERODACTYL COSTUME

How would you like to fly as high as a pterodactyl? Create your own prehistoric costume and soar as high as your imagination!

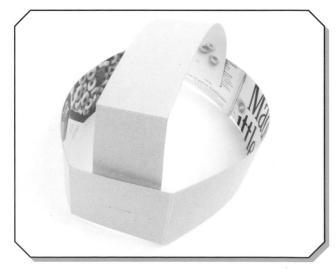

SUPPLIES

- cereal box
- scissors
- stapler
- pencil

- ruler
- cutting mat
- paint and paintbrush

- permanent markers
- duct tape
- corrugated cardboard

- drill (or hammer and nail)
- 2 pipe cleaners
- craft knife

STEPS FOR HEAD

1 Cut out two strips from a cereal box.

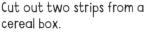

2 Staple one strip to go around your head and the other to go over your head.

3 Draw three similar-sized, connected triangles for the pterodactyl's face. Cut the triangles along the outline. Use your scissors to score the dotted connecting lines. Bend the cardboard along those lines.

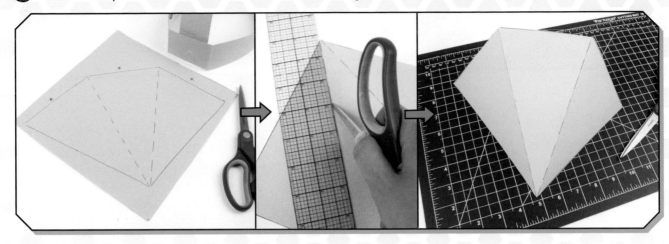

4 (To make and attach the back piece)

Cut out a piece to be the pointy back of the head.

Cut a slit at the bottom of the shape. Then bend the two created tabs opposite ways.

Cut out a slit as wide as the back shape in your headpiece.

Slide the back piece in. Staple the tabs in place.

5 Staple the face in front.

6 Paint your headpiece. Add details using permanent markers and duct tape.

Turn the page to make cool pterodactyl WINGS!

1 Cut out a rectangle from corrugated cardboard that will fit on your back.

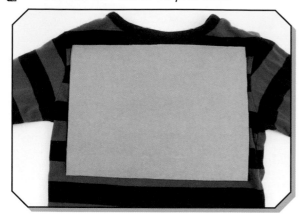

 2 Cut out this wing shape for both arms.

3 Cut out four small rectangles to act as the fasteners. Now you should have two wing pieces, four small rectangles, and one back-sized rectangle.

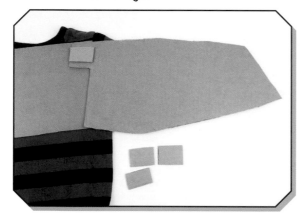

 4 Drill two holes in your back piece, one hole in each of your wings, and two holes in all four of your small rectangle fasteners.

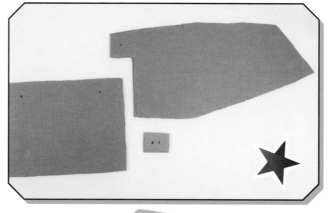

5 Practice attaching your wings to make sure your cardboard fasteners work. Repeat these steps to attach the other wing.

Slide both ends of a pipe cleaner through the two holes of a small rectangle.

Slide both ends of the pipe cleaner through the wing and the back piece.

Slide the pipe cleaner ends through the two holes of another small rectangle. Twist them together.

Straighten the wings and use a line to mark the location of your shoulders.

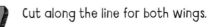 Cut along the line for both wings.

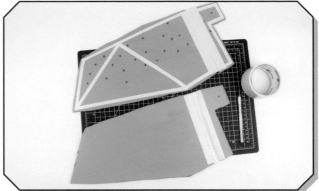

 Take everything apart and decorate your wings with paint, markers, and duct tape.

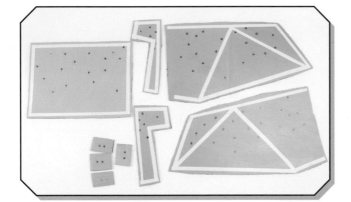

 Tape all wing pieces back together. Reattach the wings to the back piece using the fasteners (see step 5 for details.).

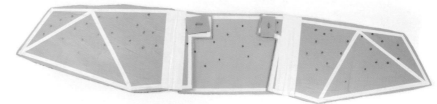

Your wings should now be able to rotate up and down, or flap front to back.

 To make your straps, cut out a long strip of duct tape. Turn it sticky-side up. Fold over one side so the strip is now half as thick. Make as many strips as you need. Use duct tape to attach two strips together to form four loops.

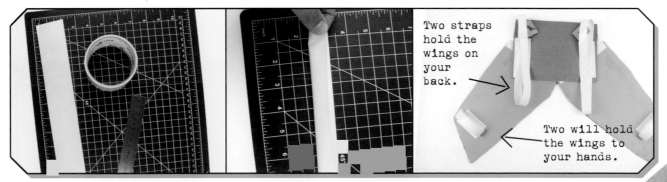

Two straps hold the wings on your back.

Two will hold the wings to your hands.

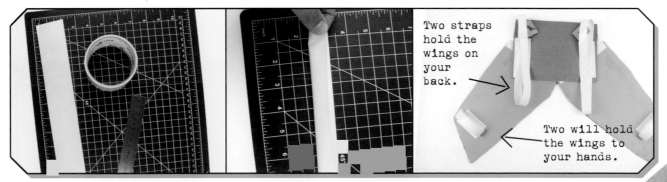

11

PREHISTORIC

PROJECT #3

TIME MACHINE

They say time only moves forward. Well, it's time to break the rules! Travel back in time with your own time machine! Which time period will you visit?

SUPPLIES

- cardboard box
- paint and paintbrush
- duct tape
- scissors
- aluminum pie plate
- pencil
- corrugated cardboard
- construction paper
- glue (glue stick, hot glue, or tacky glue)
- permanent markers
- drill
- pipe cleaner
- additional items: colander, CD covers, stickers, clothespins, baking tray, magnetic numbers, egg beaters, pushpins, CDs, string of lights

 Decorate your box with a coat of paint and strips of duct tape.

2 (To make the power meter)
Cut out a portion from your pie plate. Trace your pie plate onto a piece of corrugated cardboard. Add on a rectangle, and then cut it out. Now you have a lever! Glue construction paper over half of your lever.

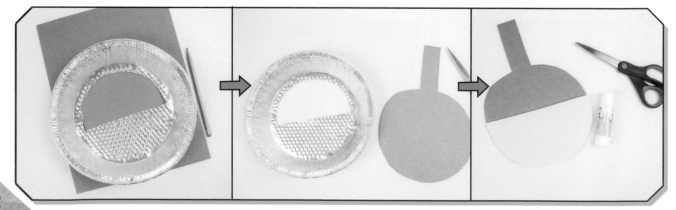

3 (To attach the power meter)

Drill two holes in the box where you want to place the power meter. Then drill two holes through the center of your pie pan and one hole through your lever. Wind the two ends of your pipe cleaner through the pie pan. Then twist the pipe cleaner. Slide the pipe cleaner through the lever. Then slide the ends through the two holes in the box. Twist the pipe cleaner ends together.

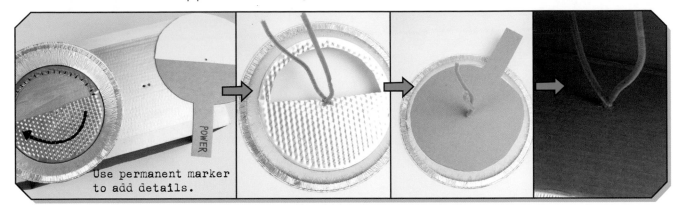

Use permanent marker to add details.

4 (To decorate your time machine)

Use a colander to hold wires.

Tape on CD covers.

Tape on a baking tray for a screen.

Add magnetic numbers to set the date.

Drill holes for items like egg beaters to sit in place.

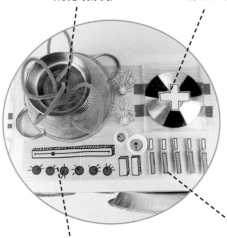

Use markers and stickers to add on details.

Decorate clothespins with duct tape.

Use pushpins to hang CDs from the box.

5 (To add lights)

Add lights by cutting out holes in the box. Then pull lights through and turn them on!

PROJECT #1
MUMMY AND SARCOPHAGUS

Ancient Egyptians were known for mummifying people and animals. Now you can create these awesome treasures for yourself!

SUPPLIES

- corrugated cardboard
- scissors
- black paint
- paintbrush
- white pencil
- masking tape
- paper towel rolls
- toilet paper rolls
- various shades of gold paint
- permanent marker

(To make a mummy)

Cut the corrugated cardboard into a mummy shape. Paint the mummy black.

Use a white pencil to draw a face, hands, and feet. Then use masking tape to "wrap" your mummy.

2 Push down on both sides of the paper towel roll to close the ends of the sarcophagus.

Paint your sarcophagus gold.

3 Add details with a marker. You can then add your mummy and close it up in your sarcophagus!

(To make mummy cats)

4 Cut out a cat shape in the front of a toilet paper roll.

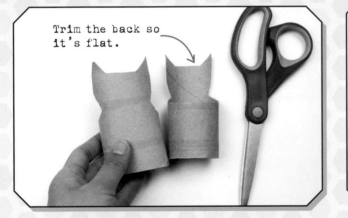

Trim the back so it's flat.

5 Place pieces of masking tape in different directions on your cat mummy.

6 Paint and use marker to add details.

PROJECT #2

PYRAMID

The ancient pyramids of Egypt are one of the most amazing wonders of the world. Ready to make one for yourself?

SUPPLIES

- large corrugated cardboard boxes
- scissors
- pencil
- duct tape
- paint and paintbrush
- permanent marker

Cut out three large isosceles triangles from your large cardboard boxes. An isosceles triangle has two sides that are the same length.

The triangles should be taller than your seated height.

TIP
No large boxes? Duct tape several cardboard sheets together to make a large enough pyramid.

Take one large triangle and trace the top portion onto a piece of cardboard. Then cut out this smaller triangle.

This will be the front of your pyramid.

Use duct tape to attach all the cardboard triangles.

Make sure to duct tape the pieces together on both the inside and outside of your pyramid.

Decorate your pyramid with paint and permanent marker.

PROJECT #3

PHARAOH HEADDRESS

Want to strut your stuff like King Tut? Now's your chance with this ultra-rad headdress worthy of all the pharaohs of Egypt!

SUPPLIES

- measuring tape
- cereal box
- ruler
- scissors
- gold and black duct tape
- craft knife
- cutting mat
- stapler

Ask an adult to measure around your head. Cut two strips from a cereal box that are a bit longer than needed to go around your head.

2 Cover the strips with gold duct tape.

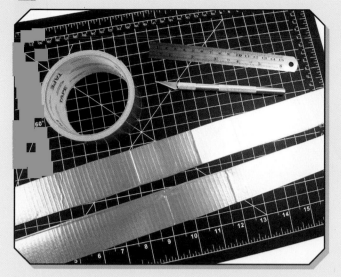

3 Staple the strips together so they create a frame that fits comfortably around your head.

4 Cut out a piece of cereal box into a half circle. This will be the front of your headdress. Cover it with strips of gold duct tape.

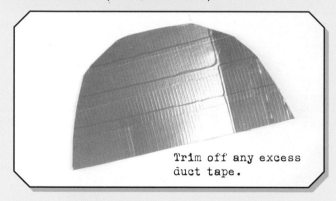

Trim off any excess duct tape.

5 Cut out two identical side pieces from your cereal box. Cover them with strips of duct tape. Trim off any excess duct tape.

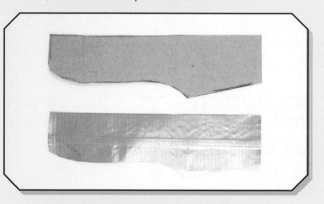

6 Tape or staple the two side pieces on. Then cut out strips of black duct tape to decorate.

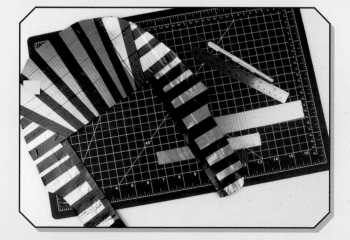

7 Once you're finished, staple the front of the headdress onto your frame. Use a strip of gold duct tape to cover the staples.

PROJECT #1
SWORD AND SHIELD

Hark all ye noble knights! Grab your swords and shields! It's time to rally behind your king and queen to protect your land and people. Let's put your cardboard crafting skills to work and create this sword and shield pair.

SUPPLIES

- paper
- pencil
- scissors
- corrugated cardboard

- duct tape (silver, gold, bronze, black)
- craft knife
- cutting mat
- tacky glue

- paint(black, red, white) and paintbrush
- permanent marker

STEPS FOR SWORD

1 Create a template for your sword and handle. Use it to trace and cut out three swords from cardboard.

2 Tape your swords together. Cut out strips of duct tape and wrap the sword's blade.

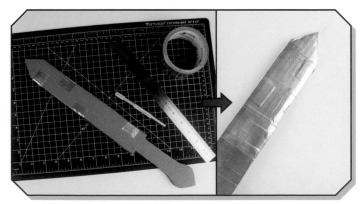

3 Now let's make the sword's guard. Cut out a rectangle with a hole in it. The hole should be large enough to fit the sword handle through. Cover it with duct tape and slide it on over your sword.

4 Now wrap the bottom of the handle with duct tape.

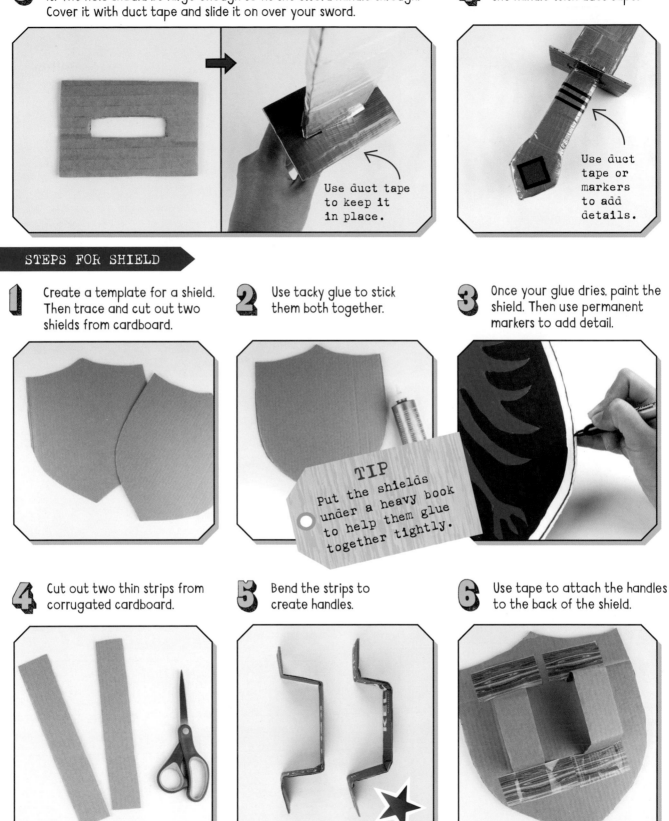

Use duct tape to keep it in place.

Use duct tape or markers to add details.

STEPS FOR SHIELD

1 Create a template for a shield. Then trace and cut out two shields from cardboard.

2 Use tacky glue to stick them both together.

3 Once your glue dries, paint the shield. Then use permanent markers to add detail.

TIP
Put the shields under a heavy book to help them glue together tightly.

4 Cut out two thin strips from corrugated cardboard.

5 Bend the strips to create handles.

6 Use tape to attach the handles to the back of the shield.

PROJECT #3

KNIGHT'S HELMET

All great knights need a strong helmet to protect them in battle. Craft your own from duct tape and cardboard in no time!

SUPPLIES

- scissors
- several pieces of cereal box cardboard
- yarn
- ruler
- duct tape
- craft knife
- cutting mat
- stapler
- pencil
- paper (for template)

Cut open your cereal box. Cut out a cardboard rectangle that is big enough to wrap around your head.

TIP

Unsure of your size? Wrap a piece of yarn around your head. Add 2 inches (5 cm) to that length. That will be the length of your cardboard piece.

2 Once you are sure of the fit, cover one side with duct tape.

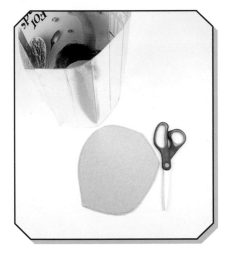

3 Curl your cardboard into a tube. Staple it together.

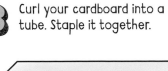

Cover the staples with small pieces of duct tape.

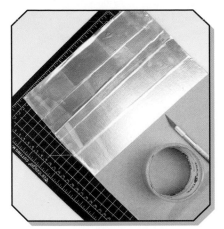

4 Trace around your cylinder on a piece of cereal box.

5 Cut out the traced shape.

6 Cover the shape with duct tape.

7 Attach the shape to the top of your helmet.

Use small pieces of duct tape to do this.

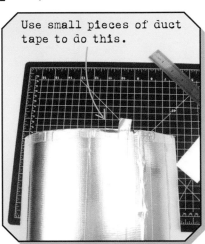

8 Cut out openings for your eyes and nose.

You can free hand this, or create your own template.

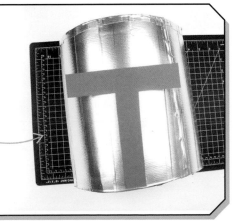

9 Add extra details with duct tape.

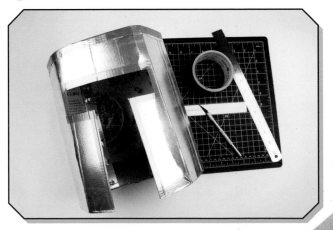

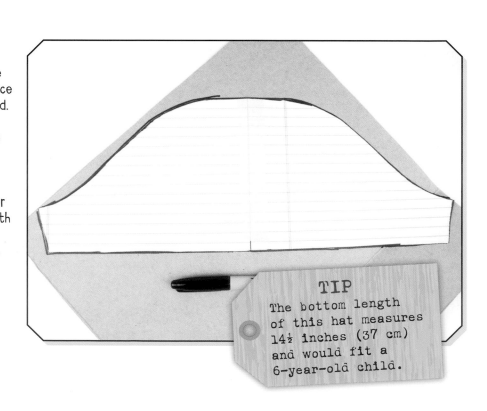

PROJECT #1

PIRATE HAT

Arrr, matey! What does every pirate need? A sturdy hat, of course! Grab some cardboard and make your own faster than you can say, "walk the plank!"

ARRR!

Measure the circumference of your head. Draw a line of the same length on paper. Then create a template for your hat with that line as the bottom.

TIP
The bottom length of this hat measures 14½ inches (37 cm) and would fit a 6-year-old child.

2 Trace your template onto a piece of cereal box cardboard two times. Cut out both pieces.

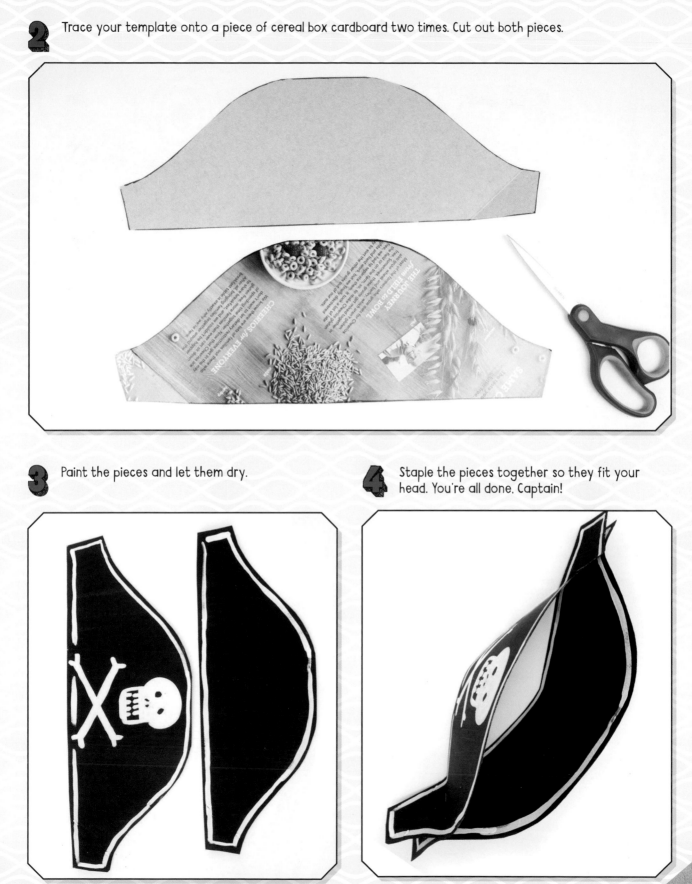

3 Paint the pieces and let them dry.

4 Staple the pieces together so they fit your head. You're all done, Captain!

PROJECT #2

AIR CANNONS

Look out there in the distance. A warring enemy ship is coming your way! It's time to ready the cannons and fight. Grab your cardboard and make your own air cannon!

- cutting mat
- scissors or craft knife
- oatmeal container
- duct tape
- permanent markers
- toilet paper rolls
- cardboard box

STEPS FOR OATMEAL AIR CANNON

 Cut a hole in the bottom of your oatmeal container.

 Duct tape the lid onto your container. Make sure there are no holes.

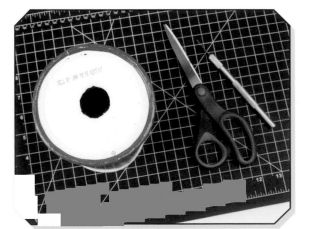

3 Use permanent markers and duct tape to add details. Decorate toilet paper rolls as targets.

Aim at your targets and give the container a firm squeeze. Watch the air knock them down!

STEPS FOR BOX AIR CANNON

1 Cut a hole in the front of your box. Tape the box closed.

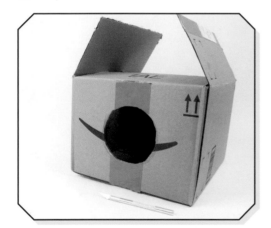

2 Make sure to seal up all corners and holes with duct tape so air can only escape through the hole.

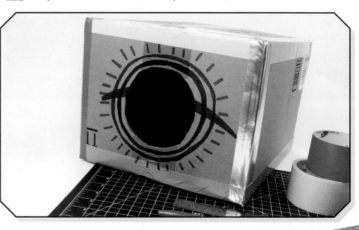

Hold the box between your hands and firmly push inward to knock your targets down with a strong gust of air!

PROJECT #3

TREASURE CHEST

Looking for a place to stash yer treasure? Grab a shoe box and some duct tape and make yourself a treasure chest fit to hold all yer loot!

SUPPLIES

- shoe box with lid
- scissors
- cereal box
- duct tape
- brown and white paint
- paintbrush

1 (To make the treasure chest lid) Cut off one of the long back panels from a shoe box lid.

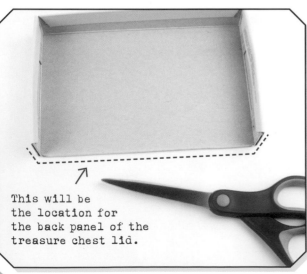

This will be the location for the back panel of the treasure chest lid.

2 Cut out two identical trapezoids from cereal box cardboard.

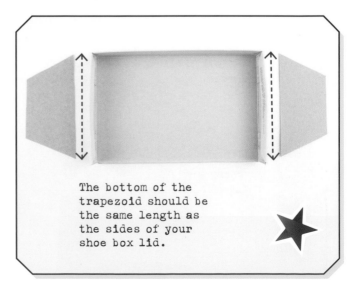

The bottom of the trapezoid should be the same length as the sides of your shoe box lid.

3 Cut out three rectangular pieces to be the top of the treasure chest. They should all be the same length as the shoe box lid.

 4 Use duct tape to assemble the top of the treasure chest. The three rectangular pieces should be sandwiched between the trapezoid pieces. The top should now sit neatly on top of the shoe box lid.

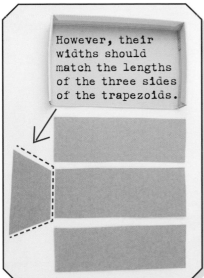

However, their widths should match the lengths of the three sides of the trapezoids.

Tape the inside of the box to hide your duct tape!

5 Paint the bottom sides of the shoe box. Then paint the sides and top of the lid.

6 Use duct tape to attach the treasure chest top to the shoe box lid. Then use duct tape to attach the back of the shoe box lid to the chest to create a "hinge." Now you have a treasure chest!

chest hinge

TIP
Short on time? You can quickly create a container to store your treasures! Simply paint an egg carton and add some gold duct tape.

29

MAKERSPACE TIPS

Download tips and tricks for using this book and others in a library makerspace. Visit *www.capstonepub.com/dabblelabresources*

READ MORE

Harbo, Christopher. *Origami Palooza: Dragons, Turtles, Birds, and More!* Origami Paperpalooza. North Mankato, Minn.: Capstone Press, 2015.

Sjonger, Rebecca. *Maker Projects for Kids Who Love Paper Engineering.* Be a Maker. New York: Crabtree Publishing Company, 2017.

Ventura, Marne. *Amazing Recycled Projects You Can Create.* Imagine It, Build It. North Mankato, Minn.: Capstone Press, 2016.

INTERNET SITES

FactHound offers a safe, fun way to find Internet sites related to this book. All of the sites on FactHound have been researched by our staff.

Here's all you do:
Visit *www.facthound.com*
Type in this code: 9781515793144

Super-cool stuff! Check out projects, games and lots more at
www.capstonekids.com

ABOUT THE AUTHOR

LESLIE MANLAPIG

Leslie is a full-time mom and sometimes puppeteer who adores books, donuts, and the color yellow. She's always on the lookout for new ways to play and make things with kids. You can read about her family's creative and crafty adventures on her blog www.PinkStripeySocks.com.

Dabble Lab Books are published by Capstone Press,
1710 Roe Crest Drive
North Mankato, Minnesota 56003
www.mycapstone.com

Cataloging-in-Publication Data is available
on the Library of Congress website.
ISBN 978-1-5157-9314-4 (library binding)
ISBN 978-1-5157-9317-5 (eBook PDF)

Editorial Credits
Anna Butzer and Shelly Lyons, editors;
Aruna Rangarajan, designer;
Tracy Cummins, media researcher;
Tori Abraham, production specialist

Image credits: All photos by Leslie Manlapig and
Enrico Manlapig, except the following: Shutterstock:
abeadev, Design Element, Africa Studio, 3 (hand, phone),
Jakub Krechowicz, Design Element, KannaA, Design
Element, Kiselev Andrey Valerevich, Design Element,
KsanaGraphica, Design Element, Patrick Foto, Back Cover,
16 (girl), Picsfive, Design Element, Raksha Shelare, 18 (boy),
Winai Tepsuttinun, Back Cover (box), Design Element

Printed and bound in the United States of America.
010750S18